Who's Afraid of ™

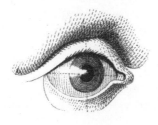

Punctuation?

There must, as we know, be a comma after every move, made by men, on this earth.

James Thurber

Editorial assistant: Mark Williams

Published in Great Britain in MMXIII by
Book House, an imprint of
The Salariya Book Company Ltd
25 Marlborough Place, Brighton BN1 1UB
www.salariya.com
www.book-house.co.uk

HB ISBN-13: 978-1-908973-48-1

1 3 5 7 9 8 6 4 2

A CIP catalogue record for this book is available
from the British Library.
Printed and bound in India.
Printed on paper from sustainable sources.

Visit
www.salariya.com
for our online catalogue and
free interactive web books.

Who's Afraid of ™ Punctuation?

It's easy, really!

Stephen Haynes

SALARIYA
BH
BOOK HOUSE

No iron can pierce the heart with such force
as a period put just at the right place.

Isaac Babel

Sometimes you get a glimpse of a semicolon
coming, a few lines farther on, and it is like
climbing a steep path through woods and
seeing a wooden bench just at a bend in the
road ahead, a place where you can expect to sit
for a moment, catching your breath.

Lewis Thomas

You practically do not use semicolons at all.
This is a symptom of mental defectiveness,
probably induced by camp life.

George Bernard Shaw, writing to T. E. Lawrence

Yesterday Mr. Hall wrote that the printer's
proof-reader was improving my punctuation
for me, & I telegraphed orders to have him
shot without giving him time to pray.

Mark Twain

Contents

Preface

*I*N A TEXT to a friend you can write however you like, but there are some situations – such as applying for a job, or writing an essay or report – where you need to make a good impression on others. This book, and others in the series, will help you to write in a way that teachers, employers and people in authority will approve of.

Unfortunately, punctuation habits vary from one country to another. What we describe here mainly applies to British English, but we do point out the most important differences between British and American usage. (Don't worry: there aren't many.) Australian and New Zealand English usually follow the British rules.

Introduction

What's the point?

PUNCTUATION is not something to be afraid of. It wasn't invented just to trip you up. The whole point of punctuation is to make what you've written easier to read. Punctuation marks are signposts that guide the reader through the words. Without them, reading would be a confusing and frustrating experience.

This book covers all the punctuation marks that are used in English – and, for good measure, a few other symbols such as numerals, and handy things like & and @. Capitals, italics and bold type are also part of punctuation, so we cover those as well. We explain when to use each symbol, and how you might be misunderstood if you don't use them in the usual way.

We cover all those awkward points, such as whether a quotation mark should go before or after a full stop; and, wherever possible, we explain the reason for the rule, because it's so much easier to remember a rule when you know the reason for it.

Pedant alert!

Look out for our **PET PEEVE** symbol. There is a certain kind of person (language experts call them *peevologists*) who loves nothing better than to pick holes in other people's use of language. 'Pet peeves' are particular mistakes (or, in some cases, so-called mistakes) which cause these people to get dangerously steamed up and, in extreme cases, write letters to the *Daily Telegraph*.

This book is not meant to turn you into a peevologist yourself – perish the thought – but it could help you to avoid needlessly provoking such people.

Punctuation trivia

Punctuation was first used in medieval manuscripts which were chanted aloud by priests or monks. Punctuation marks told them when to raise their voice at the start of a sentence, when to lower it at the end, and when to use special turns of voice to indicate a pause or a question. This made it much easier for the congregation to follow the sense of the words (which were in Latin, of course). The same symbols that were used for punctuation also developed into an early form of musical notation.

The joy of punctuation

Although we've tried to give hard-and-fast rules where possible, you'll notice that much of the guidance given in this book is fairly flexible. A dash can do many of the things that a colon can do; a pair of dashes can stand in for a pair of brackets; you have some choice over which words to hyphenate. The joy of punctuation is that it's an art as well as a science: without flouting the rules, you can develop your own style, using these various dots and squiggles to add expression to your writing. Just bear in mind that the basic purpose of these marks is to make it easier for your readers to follow your train of thought.

The basics

Think of punctuation marks as signposts to guide the reader through what you have written. When you speak to someone face to face, it's not just the words that convey your message: your pauses, the rising and falling of your voice, the expression on your face, all help the listener to understand your meaning. When you write, your reader has to manage without these clues. That's why punctuation matters: it shows the reader how you want your words to be interpreted.

A sentence begins with a capital letter and ends with a full stop, unless there's a good reason to end with an exclamation mark, a question mark or suspension points instead.

Commas, colons and semicolons divide a long sentence into shorter sections to make the meaning clearer.

Hyphens clarify meaning by showing which words belong together as a group.

What makes a sentence?

A simple sentence consists of a subject and a predicate. The subject is always a noun (a 'naming word', as my teacher Miss Cable used to say) or a pronoun (a word that stands in for a noun). At its simplest, the predicate may be nothing more than a verb (what Miss Cable called a 'doing word'), denoting the action performed by the subject. Famously, the shortest sentence in the King James Bible consists of just a subject and a verb:

Jesus wept. *(John 11.35)*

Some verbs can be accompanied by an object (a noun or pronoun naming the person or thing affected by the action):

John	loves	Mary.
subject	*verb*	*object*

In this case, the verb and the object together make up the predicate. To make a proper sentence, the verb must be a finite verb — one which agrees with the subject and is in the past, present or future tense. The verb in 'John loves' is a finite verb in the present tense; 'John loved' has a finite verb in the past tense. 'John loving' and 'John to love' are not proper sentences because the verbs are not finite — they do not have a past, present or future tense.

11

Brackets and dashes interrupt the flow of a sentence to squeeze in extra information.

Quotation marks indicate speech, or material quoted from another person.

Apostrophes indicate contractions (words which have been abbreviated by squashing them together), and also mark the possessive case; this double use causes anxiety for some people, but the rules are really not difficult.

A few other marks are worth knowing, such as the ellipsis, used to indicate material that has been omitted.

There is usually no space between the end of a word and the punctuation mark that comes after it, though we will meet a few exceptions to this rule.

Punctuation can only be explained by example, so in this book you'll often find more examples than rules. Technical terms have been used sparingly, but it's not possible or desirable to avoid them altogether; the most important ones are defined in the Glossary on pages 93–94.

Also known as: caps, upper case

Caps are used:

- **to indicate the beginning of a sentence**
- **to mark the beginning of a line of verse**
- **for the pronoun** *I*
- **to indicate a proper name**
- **to indicate personal titles**
- **in titles of publications**
- **in acronyms.**

Beginning a sentence

A sentence begins with a capital letter, whether it's a complete and grammatical sentence with subject and predicate:

Today's forecast is rain.

or a sentence fragment – a short phrase which isn't strictly a sentence but stands in for one:

Today's forecast? Rain.

The only exception is when the beginning of the sentence is missing for some reason:

'. . . rain in the north and west,' said the weather forecaster as I switched on the radio.

Beginning a line of verse

It's traditional for each line of a poem to begin with a capital, whether there is a new sentence or not; but this rule is not always followed.

The pronoun *I*

The pronoun *I* is always capitalised.

Just in case

Capital letters are sometimes described as 'upper case'; non-capitals are 'lower case'. This dates from the time when a page of print was made up from individual pieces of metal type, which were stored in type cases – drawers or trays divided into many small compartments. The capitals were kept in the upper drawer of a pair. This may sound like an urban myth, but it's the sober truth.

Proper names

Caps are used for the following kinds of names:

- names of people, including abbreviated names, nicknames and pseudonyms: John Smith, J. S., Lofty, Big Daddy

- names of places: Acacia Avenue, Burkina Faso, the People's Republic of China

- names of ships (these are usually italicised): the *Golden Hind*, RMS *Titanic*

- names of historical events: the Second World War, the Battle of Marathon (but 'battle of Marathon' is also acceptable)

- names of businesses, organisations or institutions: the Blue Boar, Impact School of Motoring (yes, really), the Department for Education

- names of commercial products or brands: Ford Ka, Fender Stratocaster, Pot Noodle.

Days of the week and months of the year are always written with caps; names of seasons usually not.

What's a proper name?

A proper name is a name that can be used to identify an individual person, place or thing: John Smith, London, France. There are, of course, thousands of John Smiths, so a proper name need not be unique to one person; but it is different in kind from a common noun like 'bricklayer' or 'ventriloquist', which refers to a whole category of people rather than an individual.

Some nouns can be common or proper, depending on how you're using them: for example, 'mum' in 'a teenage mum' is a common noun referring to a whole group of people, but 'Mum' or 'Mother' is the equivalent of a proper name when you're referring to your own parent.

Names of planets such as Mars and Saturn are always capped. With *the earth* and *the moon*, caps are optional, but if you're talking about Mars and Earth in one breath they should both be treated the same.

Names or titles with religious significance are normally capped: *God, the Lord, the Prophet*. However, it is not usual to capitalise *god* or *goddess* when referring to a pagan religion. Many people capitalise *He*, *Him* and *His* when referring to the deity, but this is not used as much as it used to be.

Adjectives derived from proper names usually take a capital letter as well: *German*, *Liverpudlian*, *Freudian*, *Darwinian*. It used to be common to write things like *french window* and *french chalk* with lower-case letters (because these things do not necessarily actually come from France), but a capital is now usual.

Personal titles

Titles such as *Mr*, *Ms*, *Miss*, *Mrs*, *Dr* are always capitalised. Other titles are capitalised when they are placed immediately before the person's name – *Prince Charles*, *President Obama* – but in other contexts lower case is permissible: *Charles, prince of Wales*; *Mr Obama, the US president*.

Book titles

Titles of books, plays, films, etc. are usually written in italics, with capitals on the first word and all the other important words: *The Power and the Glory*, *A Midsummer Night's Dream*, *The Shining*. Smaller items such as poems, or chapters in a book, are capitalised in the same way but placed in quotation marks rather than italicised. By tradition, sacred books such as the Bible and the Koran are not italicised.

Acronyms

Acronyms (abbreviations made from the initial letters of a phrase) are normally written in caps:

NATO (North Atlantic Treaty Organisation)
UAE (United Arab Emirates)
ASBO (Anti-Social Behaviour Order)

However, terms like *asbo* may be written in lower case if they have become so familiar that they are thought of as ordinary nouns.

Don't shout

Don't use caps just for emphasis. In electronic media, writing a whole phrase in caps is considered the equivalent of shouting. It doesn't look any better in print, either.

Small caps are capital letters that are roughly the same height as lower-case ones. They are often used for the abbreviations BC and AD (or BCE and CE, if you prefer). If, for any reason, you need to type a whole word or phrase in capitals, use small caps to avoid 'shouting'.

Also known as: full point, period (especially in US)

The full stop is used:

- **to indicate the end of a sentence**
- **after certain abbreviations**
- **as a decimal point**
- **as an element in a url.**

Ending a sentence

Every complete sentence should end with a full stop, unless there is a good reason for it to end with a question mark, an exclamation mark or suspension points instead:

I'm going.
Are you coming?
You're not going out like that!
Well, he said he was coming…

One exception is a sentence which is used as a name, title or heading; these don't usually have a full stop, though they may have a question mark, exclamation mark or suspension points:

Mr Smith Goes to Washington (film)
Where's Wally? (book)

On and on

Use full stops regularly; don't let your sentences run on for ever. There is no reason to be ashamed of using short sentences, and they are usually easier to read and understand than long ones.

After abbreviations

This use of the full stop is rapidly going out of fashion. In British English, full stops are no longer used with acronyms (abbreviations derived from the initial letters of a phrase, such as *NATO* from *North Atlantic Treaty Organisation*), or with personal titles such as *Mr*, *Mrs*, *Ms* or *Dr*.

When an abbreviation includes the last letter of the whole word (such as *dept* for 'department'), the full stop is optional. It's usual to do without it nowadays in abbreviations for street names, such as *Rd, St, Ave* or *Pk.*

A full stop is still used with a truncated word, such as *misc.* for 'miscellaneous', and with *a.m.* and *p.m.*

A full stop is often used after imperial units of measurement (3 ft. 6 in., 1 lb. 7 oz.), but metric units are officially written without (1.5 kg, 3 km).

Decimal point

The full stop serves to indicate a decimal:

They were an average family with 2.4 children.

It used to be common to use a dot raised above the line, but this is now considered unnecessary.

In a url

Internet and email addresses ('uniform resource locators') invariably include a dot. These have to be copied exactly, or they just won't work.

21

Question marks

The uses of the question mark are:

- **to indicate a question**
- **to express doubt or puzzlement.**

Asking a question

A question mark appears at the end of a question, and that's very nearly all there is to say about it:

Have you fed the cat yet?
Is that lipstick on your collar, dear?
What do you say to a nice cup of tea?

A rhetorical question is one that doesn't require an answer – but it still counts as a question, and needs a question mark:

What can I say? I'm thrilled.

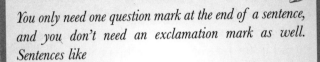

Overkill

You only need one question mark at the end of a sentence, and you don't need an exclamation mark as well. Sentences like

Did he ever explain about the sardines???!!!

are fine in a text to a friend, but don't do this sort of thing when you want to be taken seriously.

This sentence is rather like a question:

I wonder what Audrey Hepburn would have done in this situation.

You can answer it as though it were a question:

She would have put him off very politely.

But it's not actually a question, because the main clause is *I wonder . . .*, and this is not a question but a statement. It means much the same as:

I don't know what Audrey would have done.

And that's not a question, either.

23

However, it's very common nowadays for sentences like 'I wonder what Audrey would have done' to be written with a question mark. Sooner or later that may come to be regarded as correct – but for the time being you should avoid it, for fear of exciting the peevologists.

Expressing doubt or puzzlement

On a label in a museum case, you might see:

Ritual object, ?Persian, ?11th century

The question marks are a shorthand way of saying that the expert who wrote the label is not certain of the date or origin of the object. (And 'ritual object' is a shorthand way of saying that the expert doesn't actually know what the object is, either.)

In everyday writing, you might put:

John said he was going to Southampton (?).

The question mark suggests that you may have misheard or misremembered, and John may have gone to Southend or Northampton or Portsmouth instead.

The uses of the exclamation mark are:

- **to indicate surprise or indignation, loud speech or noise, or shouting.**

Surprise, indignation or loudness

An exclamation mark may be used at the end of a sentence to suggest surprise or indignation:

> Blimey! I didn't expect that!
> I say! This is most irregular!

It may also indicate loud speech or shouting:

> Ahoy there!
> Resistance is useless!

But there is no need to use more than one exclamation mark at a time, even when the shouting is excruciatingly loud.

25

In informal writing, an exclamation mark in brackets implies that the writer herself is surprised by what she has written:

Torquil actually apologised (!) for what he said the other day.

If you're indicating a loud noise of some kind – the written equivalent of a sound effect – then an exclamation mark is compulsory:

Crash! Bang! Wallop!

A bewildered cartoon character might have a thought bubble containing nothing but an exclamation mark. This doesn't really work in other kinds of writing.

Too much of a good thing

Unless you're writing an adventure story with lots of shouting and action, try not to use more than one exclamation mark per page. In a non-fiction work, two per book should be plenty. Bear in mind F. Scott Fitzgerald's comment, 'An exclamation point is like laughing at your own joke.'

Dot dot dot

Also known as: suspension points, ellipsis

Three dots are used:

- **to indicate that a sentence or phrase trails off and is left unfinished**
- **to indicate that something has been omitted from a quotation.**

Join the dots

There's more than one kind of 'dot dot dot'. When a sentence trails off, it's usual to use three dots close together; these are called suspension points. *Some computer keyboards have a special keystroke for this; on my Mac keyboard it's alt + semicolon.*

When indicating an omission, the three dots are typed with spaces before, between and after them; this is called an ellipsis. There is no short cut for this as far as I know.

27

Trailing off

Three dots, close together, are used at the end of a sentence which has been left unfinished:

'They couldn't hit an elephant at this dist...'
(allegedly the last words of Major-General John Sedgwick, US Army, 1864)

Sometimes suspension points may be used even when the sentence is complete, to suggest that there is more to be said on the subject. In this case the suspension points imply some kind of promise or threat:

Watch this space... (promise)
You'd better watch out, young man... (threat)

Leave it out

When you're quoting something said or written by someone else, you won't always want to quote it in full. An ellipsis (three dots, spaced out) shows where something has been left out:

'History is . . . bunk.'

(What Henry Ford actually said was 'History is more or less bunk.')

If you're leaving out the end of a question, don't forget to add a question mark after the ellipsis:

This book is the first in a series called 'Who's Afraid of . . . ?'

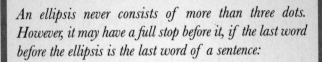

How many dots?

An ellipsis never consists of more than three dots. However, it may have a full stop before it, if the last word before the ellipsis is the last word of a sentence:

That was the first point I wanted to make. . . . Now here's my third point.

No cheating!

Don't use an ellipsis to change the meaning of a quotation – that's not fair on the original writer or speaker. It would be wrong to quote:

'Bulstrode is . . . a sensitive and expressive pianist.'

if the original sentence was:

'Bulstrode is not by any stretch of the imagination a sensitive and expressive pianist.'

29

The comma is the weakest of the punctuation marks that can be used to break up a sentence. It is used:

- **to link clauses or phrases within a sentence**
- **after an introductory phrase**
- **to reduce ambiguity**
- **in pairs, to indicate a parenthesis**
- **to separate entries in a list**
- **to separate a series of adjectives**
- **to make large numbers more legible.**

Linking clauses or phrases

If a sentence contains more than one clause, linked by a conjunction such as *and* or *or*, it is sometimes helpful to link the main clause to the subsidiary clause with a comma:

I used to like those, but I don't any more.

But the modern tendency is to leave out the comma unless there is a risk of confusion. As a rule, the shorter the clauses, the less necessary the comma. Read the sentence to yourself: if you find that it sounds natural to pause at the end of the first clause, then a comma may be in order.

A comma must *never* be used to separate two clauses which are complete sentences in their own right; this will send the peevologists into paroxysms. Complete sentences must be separated by a full stop, unless a colon or semicolon is more appropriate. (However, commas may be used when *three or more* complete, short sentences are set out as a list, as in the first example on page 38.)

A bedding shop that I pass regularly has this infuriating slogan in the window:

A third of your life is spent in bed, is it spent in comfort

The two clauses are quite separate: the first is a statement, the second a question, and each of them is a complete sentence in itself. (And as for the missing question mark – aaargh!) It would be OK to treat them as two separate sentences:

A third of your life is spent in bed. Is it spent in comfort?

But, since the two clauses are closely linked together – the first clause introducing the topic which the second clause comments on – it would be better to join them with a semicolon:

A third of your life is spent in bed; is it spent in comfort?

After an introductory phrase

If your sentence begins with an introductory phrase of some kind, a comma can be helpful to signal where the main clause – the 'meat' of the sentence – begins:

After Elizabeth I's death, James VI of Scotland became king of England.

Generally speaking, the shorter the introductory phrase, the less necessary the comma. There's no need to use a comma in this sentence, for example, though you may if you insist:

In 1603 James VI of Scotland became king of England.

But it is usual to include a comma after an adverb or adverbial phrase that modifies the sense of the whole sentence:

However, . . .
Strictly speaking, . . .
On the whole, . . .

Reducing ambiguity

Compare these two sentences:

I didn't go, because of what she said.
I didn't go because of what she said.

The first means 'I didn't go, and what she said was the reason for my not going.' The second sentence *could* mean the same, but it could also mean 'I did go, but what she said was not the reason for my going.' The comma in the first sentence makes it clear that *I didn't go* is the main clause.

Commas can act as signposts to make clear to the reader which way the sentence is heading. Here's a slightly awkward but perfectly intelligible sentence:

Those who can, get out while the going is good.

If you leave out the comma, it looks as though the main clause of the sentence is missing; the reader expects something like this:

Those who can get out while the going is good [would be well advised to do so].

Sentences which are easy to misread are known as 'garden path' sentences (from the phrase 'to lead someone down the garden path'). A 'signpost' comma can save the reader from having to backtrack and reinterpret the sentence.

To indicate a parenthesis

A parenthesis is a phrase that is inserted into a sentence to comment on it or to provide additional information. It may be placed in brackets, or between dashes, but – provided it isn't a complete clause or sentence – sometimes a pair of commas is all that's needed:

Mr Cameron, the prime minister, said the government was looking into the matter.

Here, the main clause tells us what Mr Cameron said, and the parenthesis reminds us who Mr Cameron is. It is essential to use two commas, one before and one after the parenthesis; otherwise the sentence can easily be misread:

Mr Cameron, the prime minister said the government was looking into it.

This gives the impression that you are speaking to someone called Mr Cameron, and you are telling him what the prime minister said.

He travelled to Islamabad, the capital of Pakistan, once a month.

The commas make it clear that he travelled once a month to Islamabad, and that, incidentally, Islamabad is the capital of Pakistan.

He travelled to Islamabad, the capital of Pakistan once a month.

Without the second comma, you might think he travelled only once, and that Islamabad is only occasionally the capital of Pakistan.

Note the position of the first comma in this example:

He considered going to Halifax but, in the end, he didn't.

The main clause is *He considered going to Halifax,* the subsidiary clause is *but . . . he didn't,* and the parenthesis is *in the end.* Because the conjunction *but* is part of the subsidiary clause, and not part of the parenthesis, the first comma comes after *but* – even though, in speech, you're more likely to pause slightly before *but* than after it.

It's usual to use parenthetic commas when addressing a person by their name or title:

> Tell you what, sis, let's go tomorrow.

But, for reasons unknown, the current Arden Shakespeare editions do not.

A special case: restrictive clauses

There is an important difference between these two sentences:

> The student, who had red hair, was writing a dissertation on Schopenhauer.

> The student who had red hair was writing a dissertation on Schopenhauer.

In the first sentence, the main clause is *The student . . . was writing . . .*, and the parenthesis *who had red hair* simply provides some incidental information about the student. In the second sentence, the whole phrase *The student who had red hair* is the subject of the verb *was writing*: the main point of the sentence is to tell us which student was writing the dissertation. In this case, the clause *who had red hair* is known as a 'restrictive clause', because it restricts or defines the subject of the sentence. The restrictive clause should not be separated from the subject by commas.

Restrictive clauses are easier to recognise when the subject of the verb is inanimate (not a person or animal), because in this case it's usual to use *that* in a restrictive clause and *which* in a non-restrictive one:

The essay, which was written by the dark-haired student, was about Wittgenstein.

The essay that was written by the dark-haired student was about Wittgenstein.

To separate entries in a list

Use commas between nouns or phrases in a list:

lock, stock and barrel
blood, toil, tears and sweat

The items in the list may be complete sentences in their own right:

Turn off the heat, leave the pan to cool, drain off the water and serve.

A comma should never be used to join *two* complete sentences (see page 31), but it's fine when three or more sentences make up a list.

If you wish, you can use an extra comma before the *and* or *or* at the end of the list; this is known as a 'serial comma':

lock, stock, and barrel

The serial comma before 'and' or 'or' is insisted on by some British publishers – notably Oxford University Press, who refer to it rather cheekily as the 'Oxford comma'. But in British English it's not usual to include the serial comma unless there's a risk of ambiguity, as in:

Marks and Spencer, Lilley and Skinner, and Abercrombie and Fitch

If one of the items in the list is a phrase which itself contains a comma, confusion is likely:

The guests were John Smith and Norma Pringle, two well-known artists, Jason Pratt, an up-and-coming author, and the vicar.

How many people are listed here? The only way to make it clear is to use semicolons instead of commas to mark off the groups of people:

> John Smith and Norma Pringle, two well-known artists; Jason Pratt, an up-and-coming author; and the vicar.

Now we know that four people were invited (John, Norma, Jason and the vicar), not seven (John, Norma, Jason and the vicar, plus two artists and an author).

To separate a series of adjectives

When two or more adjectives are attached to one noun, it's traditional to put commas between them:

> an evil, cantankerous, foul-smelling old shrew

Why no comma before the 'old'? Certain common, short adjectives, such as 'old' or 'little', somehow seem to attach themselves to the noun more closely than other adjectives. We're not talking about a shrew who happens to be both foul-smelling and old, but an old shrew who happens to be foul-smelling. Use a comma only where you could have used the word 'and'.

A recent newspaper report referred to 'the oldest, unambiguous evidence' for hunting by ancient humans. The comma here is just plain wrong, because the two adjectives do not have the same status: *unambiguous* tells as what kind of evidence it is, and *the oldest* tells us which piece of unambiguous evidence is being discussed. We're talking about the oldest of the unambiguous evidence, not just evidence that happens to be both unambiguous and old.

Large numbers

When writing a number of more than three digits, commas are used to mark off the digits into groups of three:

A mile equals 1,760 yards.

Dates are an exception to this rule:

As many as 2,017 such incidents were reported between 1979 and 2012.

The colon has very specific uses:

- **to introduce a list (such as this one)**
- **to introduce a clause which expands on the previous clause**
- **to introduce a speech or quotation**
- **to introduce a subtitle**
- **to indicate a ratio.**

Introducing a list

A colon draws attention to the fact that a list of items or points is about to begin:

A gun consists of three parts: lock, stock and barrel.

To make Welsh rarebit you will need the following:

- 2 slices of bread per person
- cheese, sliced or grated, enough to cover the bread
- seasoning to taste.

41

However, if the list is a short one, and is not preceded by an introductory phrase such as 'as follows', then no colon is needed:

A gun consists of lock, stock and barrel.

Don't add a dash

Decades ago, when I were a lad, we were taught to begin a list with a colon followed by a hyphen or dash:–

This looks terribly old-fashioned nowadays – don't use it unless you're old enough to call shop assistants 'Miss'.

Introducing a second main clause

The second clause can complement the first in several ways:

We eventually found out why he was late: his train had not turned up. (explanation)

He had been ill, he said: his sciatica had been playing up again. (giving additional, more specific information)

Many of the children had brought toys with them: several had teddy bears, and at least one had a panda. (giving examples)

Note that in each of these examples a full stop could have been used instead, making the two clauses into two complete sentences. But the colon is preferable because it draws attention to the relationship between the two sentences.

Keep it small

In British English the clause following the colon does not begin with a capital letter, though in US usage it may.

Introducing a speech or quotation

It's traditional to introduce a speech with a comma (see page 63), but a colon may be used instead, especially if you want to draw attention to the quotation in some way – to invite the reader to admire it, for example:

As Shakespeare said: 'All the world's a stage.'

43

Shakespeare summed it up well: 'All the world's a stage.'

In the second of these examples, because there is no introductory phrase such as 'he said', the colon is indispensable.

Subtitles

When quoting the title of a book or article, it is customary to use a colon between the main title and the subtitle (if there is one), irrespective of whether it is printed this way in the actual book:

Politics: An Introduction

Denoting a ratio or proportion

In this case the colon may be written with a space before it as well as after (ideally this should be a narrow space, if you're using a program which allows this), or with no space at all:

The sides of a golden rectangle are in the proportion $1:1.618$.

A 35 mm film negative has the aspect ratio $2:3$.

The semicolon has very few uses:

- **to link two main clauses which are closely related in meaning**
- **to separate items in a list.**

To link two related clauses

A semicolon is used between two clauses which could have been written as separate sentences, but which are so closely related that it is better to make them one sentence.

> Bert was the lively one; Edna was more thoughtful.

Here, the relationship between the two clauses is one of comparison. The semicolon could be replaced with 'while' or 'whereas'.

> War was declared; factories around the country began to make munitions.

The relationship here is cause and effect: the second clause describes what happened as a result of the event described in the first clause.

It's cold today; do you remember what it was like in the winter of 1946?

This time the first clause merely introduces the topic which is taken up in the second clause.

Don't use a semicolon where there is no real link between the two sentences:

It was a dark and stormy night. Fatima was watching the news.

These are quite separate statements, and there is no reason to link them together.

Don't use a semicolon where a colon would be more appropriate (see pages 42–43). And resist the temptation to string too many clauses together; every sentence has to end eventually.

Separating items in a list

Items in a list are normally set off by commas, but a semicolon can be used as a stronger division to avoid ambiguity (see pages 38–39).

Hyphens are used:

- **to join compound words**
- **to indicate a word break at the end of a line**
- **when writing numbers in words.**

Dashes are used:

- **to indicate a range of numbers**
- **to indicate contrast or comparison**
- **to introduce an amplification or afterthought**
- **in pairs, to indicate a parenthesis.**

Compound words

A compound is a word consisting of two or more elements, each of which is a complete word in its own right. There is an infinite number of compound words in English (literally infinite, because you can make up a new one whenever you need one), and they may be formed in many ways; here is a small selection:

- saggar-maker's bottom-knocker (two compound nouns, each made from two simple nouns)

- love-in (compound noun made from a noun (or a verb?) and a preposition)

- asset-strip (compound verb made from a noun and a verb)

- sky-blue (compound adjective made from a noun and an adjective)

- blue-collar (compound adjective made from an adjective and a noun)

- see-through (compound adjective made from a verb and a preposition)

- bog-standard (compound adjective made from two nouns)

- seven-year-old (compound adjective or noun made from a number, a noun and an adjective)

- boil-in-the-bag (compound adjective comprising an entire verb phrase).

Unfortunately, there is no standard way of writing compound words in English. Some are usually written as one word:

armchair, keepsake, ironmonger, pullover, meltdown, clodhopper, shopfront, messroom

others with a hyphen:

rumour-monger, major-general, navel-gazing, well-liked, seat-of-the-pants, wisteria-clad

and others as two separate words:

office manager, prime minister, bus driver, people carrier, shadow chancellor.

In the absence of any hard-and-fast rules, writers are often advised simply to choose a good dictionary and follow what it says. But here are a few guidelines that may help:

- The shorter the compound, the more likely it is to be written as one word.

- The more familiar and long-established the compound, the more likely it is to be one word.

- Compounds consisting of two colour adjectives take a hyphen: *blue-green, bluish-green*.

- Compound adjectives involving a number are normally hyphenated: *a two-car family, a 64,000-dollar question.*

- Compounds that are pronounced as two words – that is, with an equal emphasis on both elements – are usually written as two words.

In British English, *no-one* is often hyphenated when it means 'nobody', but definitely not when it means 'not a single', as in *No one size fits all.*

Some compound adjectives are hyphenated in all contexts:

It was a fast-flowing river.
The river was fast-flowing.

But those which are not hyphenated when they are used predicatively (after the noun) do take a hyphen when used attributively (before the noun):

It was a well-organised party.
The party was well organised.

Adverbs ending in *-ly* are usually not followed by a hyphen in any context:

The buds were fully developed.
The tree had fully developed buds.

Note the use of a space after the first hyphen in phrases like *19th- and 20th-century writers*. The *19th-* here is part of a compound adjective, so it needs a hyphen to join it to *century*; but it needs a space after the hyphen to prevent it from joining on to *and* instead. This looks a bit awkward, but it's still neater than writing '19th-century and 20th-century' in full.

Related to compound words are words that include a prefix or suffix. Prefixes are attached to the beginning of a word, suffixes to the end; they are not complete words in their own right, but modify the meaning of the words to which they are attached. Most such words are now written without a hyphen:

anticyclone, counterattack, overextended, prewar, postwar, semicircle, subsection (prefixes)

warlike, clockwise, newsworthy (suffixes)

A hyphen *may* be used if the main element of the word is a proper name, needing a capital letter, as in *anti-American*. A common exception is *transatlantic*.

Word breaks

A hyphen is used at the end of a line to indicate that a word is continued on the next line. This use of the hyphen may well be on its way out, because with modern word-processing it is usually possible to avoid word breaks. If you do need to break a word, there are a few simple rules to follow:

- Don't take over or leave behind fewer than three letters.

- If the word is a compound, break it between the two elements of the compound; don't give it an extra hyphen, as in *mind-bog-gling*.

- If the word has a clearly recognisable prefix or suffix, detach the prefix or suffix from the stem of the word: *con-template, contempt-ible*.

- If the word contains a double consonant, it's usually best to break between the two consonants: *com-motion*.

- Avoid any break that creates a misleading, offensive or unintentionally humorous word: *reap-pear, the-rapist, mil-lion*. My local paper in Essex used to make a point of hyphenating *Es-sex* at every opportunity; this is silly.

- Never end a page or column with a hyphen.

Writing numbers in full

On the rare occasions when numbers have to be written out in words, a hyphen is used between the tens and the units:

> one thousand, nine hundred and seventy-two
> (The comma after 'thousand' is optional.)

Some like to write fractions with a hyphen:

> one and three-quarters

The reason for this is a mystery to me.

En-rules and beyond

Several different lengths of hyphen and dash are available, and each has its own uses:

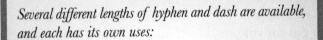

hyphen - en-rule – em-rule — 2-em rule ——

'En' and 'em' are traditional typesetting terms, derived from the width of a capital N or M. To type an en-rule on a word-processor, use alt + hyphen; for an em-rule, alt + shift + hyphen. A 2-em rule is just two em-rules.

Watch this space

Hyphens do not have a space before or after them, except in special cases such as '19th- and 20th-century' (see page 51).

When an en-rule is used to indicate a range of numbers or a contrast, it does not have a space before or after it. When used to mark a parenthesis or an afterthought, it has a space before and after.

US publishers—and a few British ones, such as Oxford University Press—use an em-rule (as in this sentence) to mark a parenthesis or afterthought; the em-rule does not have a space before or after.

A range of numbers

An en-rule, rather than a hyphen, is used to denote a range of numbers:

pages 19–21
£20,000–25,000 depending on experience
the 1914–1918 war

You can write 1930–1932, 1930–32 or 1930–2; all are correct (though different publishers have

54

their preferred house styles, and ours is 1930–1932). Numbers in the teens should never be abbreviated (always 12–13, not 12–3), and it would be very odd to break a number indicating a century (use 1899–1901, not 1899–901).

Ranges of numbers should be written either with an en-rule (1914–1918) or in words (from 1914 to 1918), never in a mixture of the two (from 1914–1918).

Pet peeve

Contrast

When two terms are being contrasted, an en-rule is used rather than a hyphen:

an actor–director collaboration
British–French relations

Note the distinction between *an actor–director collaboration* (en-rule, denoting an interaction between two different people) and *a singer-songwriter* (hyphen, denoting just one person who happens to do two things). Note also that *Franco-British relations* takes an ordinary hyphen, because *Franco-* is a prefix (an element attached to the beginning of a word), not a whole word in its own right.

Amplification or afterthought

A dash is often used to introduce an extra clause tacked onto the end of a sentence to comment on it or provide further information:

> He's writing a book about punctuation – so he says.

This is effectively the same thing as a parenthesis, and the extra material could be put in brackets if you prefer.

Parentheses

A parenthesis (see opposite) is usually enclosed in brackets, but en-rules may be used instead if preferred. Like brackets, they must be used in pairs, the second one indicating that the main sentence is about to resume:

> His plan – if it can be called a plan – is to sit tight and hope that things improve.

Ordinary brackets, also known as round brackets or (especially in American usage) parentheses, are used:

- **in pairs, to indicate a parenthesis**
- **singly, to set off items in a list of numbered or lettered points.**

Brackets ( ), square brackets [ ] and braces { } also have specialist uses in mathematics, which are beyond the scope of this book.

What's a parenthesis?

A parenthesis is a phrase – which may be anything from a single word to more than a paragraph – which is inserted into a sentence (or sometimes between sentences) to provide some kind of additional information. It need not be grammatically related to the rest of the sentence; the parenthesis interrupts the sentence, and once the parenthesis is finished the sentence continues as if the parenthesis were not there.

Indicating a parenthesis

A parenthesis always requires both an opening and a closing bracket:

> The government (in the opinion of many seasoned observers) is barking up the wrong tree.

The main clause of this sentence is *The government is barking . . .*; the parenthesis interrupts the sentence to give us additional information – in this case, the source of this opinion.

It would be odd to begin a sentence with a parenthesis, but it's perfectly acceptable to end with one:

> The government is barking up the wrong tree (this, at least, is the opinion of many seasoned observers).

Note that the final full stop goes outside the brackets, because it belongs to the main clause. And, because it's part of a larger sentence, the parenthesis does not begin with a capital letter, even though, in this case, it's a complete sentence in its own right. However, if the parenthesis comes after the main clause *and* is a complete sentence in its own right, you may punctuate it as a separate sentence if you prefer:

The government is barking up the wrong tree. (At least, this is the opinion of many experts.)

In this case the whole sentence, including its capital letter and its full stop, goes inside the brackets.

A parenthesis can be placed between dashes (en-rules) instead of brackets if you prefer:

This government – surely the least competent we have seen in years – has lost its way.

It can also be placed within commas, provided the parenthesis is not a complete sentence:

This government, surely the least competent in living memory, cannot last much longer.

It's perfectly acceptable to put a small parenthesis within a larger one:

The painting (which is thought to be the work of Alfred Sisley (1839–1899)) last came onto the market in 1937.

But in this case you could make the sentence look neater by putting the larger parenthesis between commas rather than brackets. (In US usage, square brackets are sometimes used for a parenthesis within a parenthesis.)

If the sentence contains a comma at the point where the parenthesis begins, the comma is always placed immediately *after* the parenthesis, never before:

We thought he had gone to France (as he did last year), but he turned out to be in Belgium.

In a list of numbers

A closing bracket may be used after each entry in a list of numbered or lettered points, though this possibly looks a bit quaint nowadays:

The three most popular names for boys were:

1) Albert
2) Herbert
3) Winston.

This is the only situation in which a closing bracket is used without an opening bracket.

Square brackets (known simply as 'brackets' in US English) have rather specialised uses:

- **inserting an explanation into a phrase quoted from another source**
- **indicating that a quotation has been altered or corrected.**

Adding an explanation

The report added that 'He [Molesworth] had known the defendant for many years.'

The square brackets tell us that the name was not present in the original quote, but has been added by the person who is quoting it, to make the sentence clearer to the reader.

Indicating a change or correction

Molesworth admitted that 'in the heat of the moment [he had] lost sight of the defendant'.

Molesworth actually said 'I lost sight of the defendant,' but changing *I* to *he* makes the quotation fit better into the larger sentence.

Molesworth wrote in his report: 'I didn't know w[h]at to do.'

The square brackets here tell us that Molesworth accidentally wrote *wat* but meant to write *what*.

In an academic work you might see something like this:

'I didn't know wat [*sic*] to do,' wrote Molesworth.

This means that there was a mistake in what Molesworth wrote, and the author, in the interests of historical accuracy, has quoted it just as it was written. *Sic* is Latin for 'thus', or 'just like this'. If you want to be *really, unspeakably* pedantic, you could even write:

[*sic*; *recte* what]

Recte is Latin for 'correctly'.

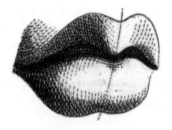

Also known as: quotes, speech marks, inverted commas

The uses of quotation marks are:

- **to indicate words which are spoken, either by a real person or by a character in a story, or quoted from another writer**
- **to draw attention to an unusual word or phrase**
- **to indicate the titles of some kinds of written work.**

Single or double?

Quotation marks can be either single ' ' or double " " . When I was at school, teachers used to call the double ones '66s and 99s'. In British English it's normal to use single quotes, except in newspapers and in handwriting. Some people may try to tell you that there's a difference in meaning between single and double quotes, but there isn't.

'Smart' quotes

Most word processors give you a choice between 'straight' or 'typewriter' quotes and 'smart' or 'curly' ones. Use the smart ones – they look much more professional.

(If you're wondering what the straight ones are for, see page 86.)

Single quotes can look a bit odd if one of the words you're quoting contains an apostrophe:

'I can't and I won't', he said.

They are positively confusing if one of the quoted words ends with an apostrophe, because this looks exactly like a closing quotation mark:

He experienced what athletes call a 'runners' high' after the race.

Neverthess, single quotes have become the norm.

But if you're quoting someone who's quoting someone else, then you use double quotation marks for the quote within a quote:

'John said, "Come in!"' said Lisa.

(US usage is the other way round: ordinary quotes are double, quotes within a quote single.)

Quoting spoken or written words

Use quotation marks only when you're repeating the actual words that someone has spoken or written:

'I'm going,' said Dad. ('I'm going' were the actual words that he used.)

Dad said he was going. (No quotes, because 'he was going' were not his actual words.)

Admiral Byng was executed, according to Voltaire, 'to encourage the others'. (Voltaire actually wrote 'to encourage the others', but he didn't write 'Admiral Byng was executed' – that's only a paraphrase of what he wrote.)

Phrases like 'she said' or 'the doctor explained' are not included within the quotation marks, because they are not part of what was said:

Professor Choudhury said, 'The problem is lack of funding.'

'The problem is lack of funding,' complained Professor Choudhury.

'The problem', declared Professor Choudhury, 'is lack of funding.'

Commas and colons

If the 'she said' phrase comes first, it's usual to introduce the quote with a comma:

The dentist said, 'Open wide.'

But you can use a colon if you prefer:

The dentist said: 'Open wide.'

If the 'she said' phrase comes at the end, then the quotation ends with a comma:

'Open wider,' urged the dentist.

And, if you put it in the middle, you will need commas in both places:

'It would help', expostulated the dentist, 'if you could open it wider than that.'

Stealing words

When you're quoting from a written work, it's important to make clear which words are quoted and which are not. Otherwise you may be suspected of plagiarism – the offence of passing off someone else's work as your own.

Long quotes

If you're quoting more than one paragraph of a book (or more than one verse of a poem), it's traditional to put an extra opening quote at the beginning of each verse or paragraph as a reminder. But it's usually better to set out long quotations in a different style – such as in smaller type – and in this case no quotation marks are needed. Don't forget to acknowledge the source of the quote.

If you're quoting only a single word, or a short phrase which is obviously not a complete sentence, no introductory comma is needed:

> The government threatened a 'rigorous crackdown' on protestors.

You also don't need the comma if you're not using a 'she said' phrase, even if what you're quoting is a complete sentence:

'All cows eat grass' is a mnemonic used in learning to read musical notation.

In this book I don't always use a comma or colon when I'm presenting a sentence by way of example; but, if I were writing dialogue, I would use commas in the traditional way.

Inside or out?

The comma after a 'she said' phrase is not part of the quote, so it stays outside the quotation marks. But what about a comma or full stop at the end of a quote? It depends on whether the punctuation is part of the quoted sentence:

'It would help', she said, 'if you would open it wider.'

What the dentist actually said was: 'It would help if you would open it wider.' So the comma after *help* is not part of the quote, and it stays outside the quotation marks. But the full stop at the end is part of what the dentist said, so it goes inside the closing quote. It's a general rule that if the quoted material is a complete sentence, or even if it looks as though it might be a complete sentence, the full stop should go inside the closing quote.

On the other hand:

> 'It would help, I think,' said the dentist, 'if you could try not to scream.'

In this case her actual words were: 'It would help, I think, if you could try not to scream.' So the comma after *I think* is part of the quoted material, and goes inside the quotation marks.

When only a single word or short phrase is quoted, the comma or full stop stays outside the quotes because it is not part of the quoted word or phrase:

> The whole affair had been 'a disaster', the spokesman admitted.

> The spokesman admitted the whole affair had been 'a disaster'.

When the 'she said' phrase comes after the quotation, there's another refinement:

> 'This tooth is dead,' said the dentist.

In this case, what the dentist actually said was: 'This tooth is dead.' This is a complete sentence, so it would normally end in a full stop. But because this isn't the end of the larger sentence (the sentence that ends with *dentist*), we replace the full stop with a comma; and the comma goes inside the quotation marks, because there was a punctuation mark here in the original sentence.

The same applies with a colon or semicolon. If you want to quote just the first half of the sentence 'Time flies like an arrow; fruit flies like a banana,' then you replace the semicolon with a comma, inside the quotation marks:

'Time flies like an arrow,' said the philosopher.

But, if you want to quote the whole sentence, you have the option of retaining the semicolon, like so:

'Time flies like an arrow,' said the philosopher; 'fruit flies like a banana.'

(US usage is much simpler: the full stop or comma goes inside the quotation marks, whether it's part of the quoted phrase or not.)

Questions and exclamations

If you're quoting a question or an exclamation, then the question mark or exclamation mark is part of the quotation and goes inside the quotation marks:

He asked, 'What's up?'

'What's up?' he asked. (Note that we don't need a comma as well as a question mark.)

'I say!' she protested.

If the larger sentence is a question but the quoted sentence is not, then the question mark is part of the main sentence and goes outside the quotes:

Did she say, 'Here I am'? ('Did she say . . . ?' is a question, but 'Here I am' is not.)

It's possible to imagine a case where the quoted sentence and the main sentence are both questions:

Did he say, 'What's up?'

In theory this sentence ought to have two question marks, one inside the quotation marks and one outside, but that would be overkill. Just keep the one inside.

And what if the quoted sentence is a question and the larger sentence is an exclamation, or vice versa? It's best to leave out the exclamation mark – they're hardly ever necessary.

Drawing attention to a word or phrase

You may want to draw attention to a word or phrase for a variety of reasons (note that in all of these cases no introductory comma is needed):

• to indicate an unfamiliar word, or one that needs explanation:

Aunt Em showed me how to make 'bonkers', which was her word for firelighters made out of newspaper.

• to indicate a word or phrase that the writer does not entirely approve of:

This is a place where teenagers like to 'hang out'. (In this case the quotation marks mean something like: 'This is a phrase I wouldn't use myself, you understand.')

• to imply that a word is being used loosely or metaphorically:

She learned to walk by holding on to the dog's tail. This 'handle' helped her to stay upright.

- in newspaper headlines, to indicate that the information given has not been verified. You'll often see something like:

ELECTRICIAN 'KILLED LOVER'

This means: 'An electrician has been accused of killing her lover, but you can't sue us for libel because we haven't actually stated that she did so.'

Quoting titles

The usual rule is that a book title is italicised, but something which is only part of a book – a poem, an article, a chapter, for example – is placed in quotation marks:

John Bunyan, *The Pilgrim's Progress* (whole book)
John Donne, 'The Flea' (short poem)

Scary!

When quotes are used to insinuate that a word is not being used properly, they are often referred to as 'scare quotes', or even 'sneer quotes':

This 'government' should resign immediately.

The writer of this sentence is trying to imply that the government is so inept that it doesn't even deserve to be called a government. Don't use quotes in this way if you want to be taken seriously.

It's definitely not a good idea to use quotes just for emphasis. You'll often see it on greengrocers' signs:

LOOK "TOMATO'S"*

These quotes look like scare quotes and give entirely the wrong impression: that those red things on sale are not real tomatoes.

On the other hand, a shop in Brighton advertises 'SOYA "MILK"', which is correct (since the product in question is not actually milk) and commendably honest.

* For the 'greengrocer's apostrophe', see page 83.

Apostrophes are used:

- **to indicate omitted letters**
- **to indicate possession.**

What could be simpler?

Omitted letters

Contractions – words that have been telescoped into a shorter form – are a distinctive feature of idiomatic English. The commonest contractions are those in which two words have been squashed into one:

- isn't, aren't, wasn't, weren't, doesn't, etc.
- I'm
- you're, we're, they're
- he's, she's, it's (standing for *it is* or *it has*)
- I've, we've, you've
- I'll, we'll, you'll, they'll.

'Smart' apostrophes

On the computer, apostrophes, like quotation marks, come in 'straight' and 'smart' forms. Use the smart form for apostrophes and the straight form for primes (see page 86).

Contractions of yesteryear

In older books you may find words with more than one apostrophe in them, such as sha'n't *for 'shall not', in which the first apostrophe stands for the missing* ll *and the second for the missing* o; *the modern spelling is* shan't.

Others that you'll meet only in historical contexts include foc's'l *(accommodation in the bow of a ship, now spelt 'forecastle'),* ha'penny *('halfpenny') and (a favourite word of my Dad's)* ha'p'orth *('halfpennyworth').*

'Tis and 'twas are rare examples of contractions that begin with an apostrophe. If you type these on a computer, it will usually convert the apostrophe automatically into an opening quotation mark. The easiest way to get round this is to type a pair of quotation marks – ''tis – and then delete the first one.

Don't use an apostrophe to indicate the missing syllables in abridged words like cello *or* fridge; *these are now regarded as perfectly proper words in their own right.*

Another use of omitted letters is to indicate a non-standard or dialect pronunciation:

> I'm 'Enery the Eighth I am, I am.
> Huntin', shootin' and fishin'.

This sort of thing should not be overdone. (For a prize example of how to overdo it, read Bram Stoker's *Dracula*.)

The possessive apostrophe

Most English nouns have four different forms:

> son, sons, son's, sons'
> berry, berries, berry's, berries'

As luck would have it, three of these forms are pronounced alike but spelt differently, so if you want to get them right you have to know the rules. Fortunately, there are only two basic rules.

1. The first rule is that the apostrophe denotes possession. If you want to say that something belongs to someone, or is part of something, or is intimately bound up with something, you use an apostrophe – and the name of the thing that belongs normally comes straight after the noun with the apostrophe:

77

the boy's book (the book belonging to the boy)

the girl's hand (the hand that is part of the girl)

the river's course (the course that is natural to the river)

If you're not talking about possession or belonging, you don't use an apostrophe:

The books were in the library. (The *s* on the end of *books* makes it plural – it means 'more than one book' – but we're not talking about anything that belongs to the books, so there's no apostrophe.)

The professor's books were on her desk. (Again, *books* has no apostrophe because we're not talking about anything that belongs to the books; but *professor's* has an apostrophe because we are talking about the books that belong to her.)

The books' spines were damaged. (This time *books'* does have an apostrophe, because we're talking about the spines that are part of the books.)

2. The second rule is that the position of the apostrophe depends on whether the noun is singular or plural:

the professor's house (Placing the apostrophe before the *s* indicates that *professor* is singular – the house belongs to just the one professor.)

the professors' house (Placing the apostrophe after the *s* indicates that *professor* is plural – at least two professors own the house between them.)

To put it another way, a plural *s* is joined directly onto the noun, but a possessive *s* is separated from the noun by an apostrophe.

These two simple rules will see you right about 90% of the time. But English is not a tidy language and there are a few complications...

Some nouns are spelt differently in the singular and plural:

cherry/cherries, story/stories, mass/masses

And the same difference applies in the possessive:

79

the baby's cot (one baby)
the babies' cots (more than one)

What if the noun already ends with an *s*, even in the singular? Usually, you add another *s* (with an apostrophe, of course) to make the possessive: *James's wife*.

A common exception is *for goodness' sake*; this set expression is normally written without the extra *s*, because (a) it's not pronounced with an extra *s* and (b) it would look awkward with four *s*'s in a row.

With classical names like Demosthenes or Herodotus you can choose whether to add a second *s* or not: *Demosthenes' speeches* and *Demosthenes's speeches* are both OK, but it looks neater without the extra *s*, don't you think?

Some nouns have a plural form which doesn't end in *s*; *children, people, brethren*. In this case the apostrophe goes before the possessive *s*, as usual: *the children's clothes*.

A few nouns have two plural forms. The plural of *person* is usually *people*, but *people* also has its own plural form, *peoples* (referring to different populations or nationalities). So there's a distinction between *the people's will* (the will of the people) and *the peoples' territories* (the territories occupied by the different peoples).

Some proper names of places or institutions are officially written without a possessive apostrophe, even though they should logically have one. (Sometimes this is because the institution was founded before the 17th century, when the possessive apostrophe came into use.) There is no rule about these exceptions – you just have to know them. Birmingham City Council caused outrage in 2009 by removing apostrophes from street names such as St Pauls Square (barbarians!).

Pet peeve

Possessive pronouns usually don't take an apostrophe: *his, hers, its, ours, yours, theirs.* Exceptions: *one's, someone's, somebody's, nobody's.*

A real oddity

In a phrase such as the king of Spain's daughter, *the possessive* s *(with its apostrophe) goes after* Spain. *Logically it ought to go after* king *instead (as in the old ballad 'The Bailiff's Daughter of Islington'), but to a modern ear this sounds even stranger.*

81

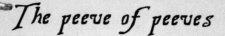

The peeve of peeves

Misuse of the apostrophe is the greatest of all punctuational shibboleths; it really gets the peevologists' goat. Bookmark these two pages, stick them on the wall, tattoo your forehead with them (well, perhaps not).

1. Never confuse the following homophones (words that sound alike):

its (belonging to it)
it's (it is *or* it has)

there (in that place)
their (belonging to them)
they're (they are)

where* (in what place)
were (past tense of *are*)
we're (we are)

whose (belonging to whom)
who's (who is *or* who has)

your (belonging to you)
you're (you are)

* *Whether these three count as homophones depends on where you come from.*

82

2. Never use an apostrophe with a plural *s* when there is no possession involved:

APPLE'S, TOMATOE'S, CRES'S

This has become known as the 'greengrocer's apostrophe' because it's such a familiar sight on handwritten notices among the fruit and veg. I assume that greengrocers are highly educated people who understand the value of advertising and know that a stray apostrophe will always get them noticed.

When not to use an apostrophe

When should you use an apostrophe before a plural *s*? Never – well, almost never:

- with numbers, such as *1930's*? – no

- with acronyms, such as *DVD's*? – no

- with words ending in a vowel, such as *volcano's*? – no, nowadays always *volcanoes*

- with a single-letter word, as in *dotting the i's and crossing the t's*, or one that just looks unfamiliar in the plural, as in *do's and don'ts*? – well, OK, here an apostrophe can be tolerated because the word might otherwise be misread.

This final section describes a few less common symbols, and other typographical features that are not actually punctuation marks but are an important part of how a well-written text is presented.

The oblique *(also called: solidus, slash, forward slash)* **and the vertical**

The oblique is used to denote alternatives, as in *and/or*, *either/or*. It is used in a few abbreviations, such as *c/o* for 'care of'.

It is occasionally used to indicate a range of numbers, especially when this consists of two adjacent numbers (12/13), though it is now more usual to use an en-rule. Historians use an oblique to indicate old-style and new-style dates: 4 February 1652/3.

The opposite of the oblique, the 'backslash' (\\), is used only in computing contexts.

84

If you are quoting a passage of verse and don't want to set it out in separate lines, use either obliques or verticals to indicate the line breaks:

Hamlet has to decide whether 'to suffer | the slings and arrows of outrageous Fortune'.

Other symbols

The ampersand, most commonly written &, is now scarcely used except in the names of businesses. It is no longer used to stand for 'and' in ordinary text.

The 'at' symbol @ used to be used only in commerce to indicate the unit price of goods:

12 loaves @ 6d. each

It has now, of course, become an essential element in email addresses.

Mathematical symbols in general are beyond the scope of this book, but it may be worth mentioning the use of the multiplication sign when giving measurements: '2 metres long by 1 metre wide' may be written as '2 x 1 m'. Strictly speaking, this should be a proper 'times' symbol, not a letter x.

Primes, which look like straight apostrophes, can be used to indicate feet and inches; for example, 3 ft. 6 in. can be written as 3′ 6″ (though nowadays the longer form is preferred). They can also indicate minutes and seconds.

Italics, bold and underlining

Italics can be used for emphasis; use them sparingly, or the effect will be lost:

It wasn't *what* he said – it was *how* he said it.

They are used for unfamiliar foreign words:

The typical dwelling of Russian peasants in the 19th century was a simple hut or *izba*.

But don't use them for words which have become naturalised in English, such as 'café' or 'garage' or 'haute couture'.

Italics are often used to draw attention to technical terms, especially when the writer is offering a definition or explanation. It's usual to italicise such words at the first mention only:

The *supertonic* is the second degree of a musical scale. In the key of C major, the supertonic is D.

When citing the scientific name of a plant or animal, it's compulsory to put the genus and species names in italics, with the genus capitalised and the species lower case:

European ash (*Fraxinus excelsior*)

Italics are used for the title of a book, but the title of a work which is only part of a book is given in quotation marks instead:

Wordsworth's poem 'Daffodils' appeared in his *Poems in Two Volumes* of 1807.

But, by tradition, religious works such as the Bible and the Koran are not italicised.

Names of ships are usually italicised: HMS *Bounty*, *Queen Elizabeth 2*.

If you're writing a whole sentence in italics, then words which would normally be italicised should go in roman type instead. You'll find examples of this in the panel on page 81.

Bold type is used only for headings or when special emphasis is required. In technical books it might be used to signal words which are defined in a glossary.

Underlining is what old-fashioned typewriters have instead of italics. It's now used only for special purposes, such as when quoting a passage from a document which has underlining in the original.

Numerals

Publishers have different rules about whether numbers should be written in words or figures. If you're writing for publication, ask your editor what rule you should follow. If not, decide for yourself which numbers should be spelt out, and be consistent.

A common rule is to write the numbers 1–10 in words, but if a large and a small number appear together, treat them both the same – 'ten or 11' just looks odd. Numbers used with a unit of measurement will normally be in figures; some publishers like people's ages to be in figures also.

Vague numbers such as 'thousands' are best given in words; 'tens of thousands' can't be written any other way.

Avoid beginning a sentence with a numeral:

1588 was the year of the Spanish Armada.

Instead, use one of these:

Fifteen eighty-eight was the year of the Spanish Armada. (awkward)

The year 1588 saw the launch of the Spanish Armada. (cumbersome)

The Spanish Armada was launched in 1588. (prosaic but impeccable)

For commas in large numbers, see page 40. For ranges of numbers, see pages 54–55.

Footnote cues

Footnotes or endnotes may be numbered in various ways: continuously throughout the book, continuously throughout each chapter (the usual method in academic books), or starting again at number 1 on each page. The cues in the text are normally presented as superscript numbers:

It has now been convincingly demonstrated that this was not the case.[6]

6. *The most detailed summary of the evidence in English is J. Robinson,* The Fosdyke Affair Re-Examined *(Cambridge, 1987), 38–47.*

Note that the footnote cue goes after any punctuation mark, with the exception of a dash or ellipsis.

If the book or paper you are writing has very few footnotes – preferably no more than one per page – asterisks may be used instead of numbers. There is also a traditional series of footnote symbols which nowadays has only curiosity value:

* (asterisk)
† (dagger, obelus or obelisk)
‡ (double dagger)
§ (section mark)
|| (parallels)
¶ (paragraph mark or pilcrow).

Don't take our word for it

If you're writing an essay for school or college, you should be given instructions on how to present references, and these should include special rules for citing online sources. Follow these instructions if they differ from the examples given here. You may well be instructed to use the Harvard system, in which book or article titles are abbreviated in the style (Brown 1884: 26–7)*; this greatly reduces the number of footnotes needed.*

Diacritics

Diacritical marks, otherwise known as accents, are used less in English than in any other European language. Almost the only time they are used with native English words is to indicate the pronunciation of words such as *blessèd*; but they do appear in a number of foreign words which have been naturalised into English, such as *café* and *façade*. (*Facade* without the cedilla is one of my personal pet peeves.)

Pet peeve

When quoting foreign words, especially names, do make every effort to include all necessary diacritics; leaving off the accent is tantamount to writing the wrong letter. (There are exceptions: in French, for example, it's correct to omit accents (but not cedillas) from capital letters.) At the very least, check in Wikipedia; it may not be the world's most reliable source of information, but it does tend to be scrupulous about diacritics.

Bullets

Bullets • are useful for setting out a list of items in easily remembered form; you will find many examples in this book. If the entries in a bulleted list are not complete sentences, there is no need to give them capital letters or full stops – though it's no bad thing to place a full stop after the last item in the list, so the reader can see that the list is complete and does not continue over the page. If all the items in the list are complete sentences, punctuate them accordingly.

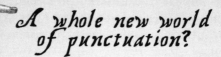

A whole new world of punctuation?

Is punctuation dying out? I'd say that rumours of its demise are exaggerated. The fact that people get aeriated about the greengrocer's apostrophe – and even write bestselling books about punctuation and pandas – suggests that it's not going to disappear in our lifetime. Indeed, a whole new set of expressive marks – the smileys – are now in everyday use, and they can convey nuances of expression that traditional punctuation marks can't. It's true that at present they are only used in informal contexts, but this may not always be the case. Perhaps one day we'll get messages from the bank saying:

We regret to inform you that your account is overdrawn :-(

Till then, let's hope that careful writers continue to see the point of punctuation.

adjective A 'describing word' used with a noun or pronoun to describe one of the characteristics of the person or thing referred to.

adverb A 'describing word' used with a verb to say how something is done. Most English adverbs end in *-ly*.

clause A sequence of words, consisting of a subject and a predicate, that is part of a larger sentence.

common noun Any noun that is not a proper noun.

conditional clause A subordinate clause introduced by *if*.

conjunction A linking word such as *and*, *or*, *but*, *yet* or *while*.

ellipsis The leaving out of a word or phrase; also, a punctuation mark (. . .) indicating that a word or phrase has been left out.

finite verb A verb that has a subject and a tense, and can form part of a main clause.

main clause The most important clause in a sentence, which could stand by itself as a sentence in its own right if the rest of the sentence were removed.

noun A 'naming word' that refers to a person, thing, place or concept.

object A noun or pronoun that names the person or thing to which the action denoted by the verb is done.

parenthesis (plural: **parentheses**) A phrase which is not grammatically related to the rest of the sentence, but is inserted into it as an interruption. It is usually placed in brackets, which themselves are sometimes known as *parentheses*.

phrase A group of words which are connected together but do not amount to a clause.

possessive case The form of a noun or pronoun that indicates possession or belonging.

predicate The part of a clause that is not the subject; it always contains a finite verb, and it also contains the object, if the verb has an object.

pronoun A word that stands in for a noun, to avoid repetition; examples include subject pronouns (*I, he, she,* etc.), object pronouns (*me, him, her*), possessive pronouns (*my, his, her*) and demonstrative pronouns (*this, these, that, those*).

proper noun The name of a particular person, thing, place, etc.

sentence A sequence of words, consisting of at least a subject and a predicate, that is sufficient by itself to form a statement or question.

sentence fragment A group of words, or a single word, that does not have all the features of a sentence but can nevertheless be understood as a statement or question: *'Tea?' 'Please.'*

subject A noun or pronoun that names the person or thing carrying out the action denoted by the verb.

subordinate clause A clause that provides additional information but cannot stand by itself as a main clause. It is typically introduced by a conjunction such as *if, when, which* or *although*.

verb A 'doing word' that names an action.

word The smallest bit of language that can be used by itself with an identifiable meaning.